RIVERS

OF

GOD

Russell Walden

DEDICATION

To my wife, Kitty. Without you,
none of this would be possible.

CONTENTS

ACKNOWLEDGMENTS

Acknowledgement to Apostle Ricardo Watson, a faithful son in the Lord. The 2018 Camp Meeting was the seed bed for this message and for that I thank you.

CHAPTER ONE

INTRODUCTION

In this series of teachings, I am going to show you the significance of the many times and places where Jesus chose bodies of water to make certain things about Himself and His plan for man known to those around Him at the time and to us through their testimony. You will see Jesus intends for you to see that you have a well on the inside of you and also a river. In fact, you have more than one river inside of you, and those rivers have specific names that communicate understandings to you of God's blessing and benefit in your life. You will see that there is an atmosphere of God's presence described as His cloud of glory, out of which precipitation from heaven is poured out upon your person and your life. There is, in fact, the rain of God distilling and falling from heaven on the inside of you at all times and in all places to refresh and strengthen you and make you fruitful. You will also find there is a pool of God's Spirit on the inside of you that the angel of His presence will come to stir the waters of your soul from time to time to bring healing and deliverance to your life. You will find again that there are rivers plural flowing out of you, out of your inner man, into your life for specific reasons to cause your life to look like "as in heaven so on earth." We will identify these rivers, and we will name them to help you understand how to release them by your faith and see them produce in your life a level of grace and breakthrough you may not have experienced heretofore.

JESUS ON THE GREAT DAY OF THE FEAST:

In John 7:37-38 we find Jesus in the temple crying out with a loud voice, making a divine and sovereign overture to all those that would come to Him as Lord and Savior:

John 7:37-38

37 -- In the last day, that great day of the feast, Jesus stood and cried, saying, If any man thirst, let him come unto me, and drink. 38 He that believeth on me, as the scripture hath said, out of his belly shall flow rivers of living water.

The timing that Jesus chose for this announcement was the Feast of Tabernacles. This is the feast that came AFTER Pentecost. In other words "after Pentecost - what next?" Do we just all speak in tongues till Jesus comes? Jesus is saying when the

FIRE FALLS on your personal Pentecost there will be and you should expect following that, a flowing out of the inside of you what constitutes currents of His purpose and His glory to reframe and reshape your life according to His purpose. Now notice that Jesus says out of your belly will flow rivers of living water. That phrase is pregnant with meaning for us that we will explore. What is your belly? Why didn't He say "out of your heart?" What are the rivers? What is the living water and what does its presence in your life promise you or produce in you? Notice again, that He doesn't just speak of a river (singular) but of RIVERS (plural). I will show you that these rivers and the reference to multiple rivers is not just something said by poetic license but something very specific, of the Spirit of God on the inside of you that once understood will have a radical impact upon your life, and how you pray, how you live and to what degree you see on a daily basis the manifest glory of God in its fullness.

God speaks often of Himself, and His son and His Spirit in terms of water and bodies of water in their particular manifestations. In introducing this body of teachings we want to go back through several chapters in the gospel of John to consider this. We will see how Jesus for a period of days travels from one body of water to the next body of water to show us something of Himself, and having laid that groundwork of understanding we will go on in the subsequent chapters and teachings to go deeper into these waters to gain knowledge and revelation beyond what you may have ever considered when reading these passages previously.

JESUS WITH THE WOMAN AT THE WELL:

In John chapter 4 Jesus interacts with a Samaritan woman at a well in her village. His disciples are gone at thc cnd of a long day's walk with thc assignmcnt to return with food to strengthen them while Jesus remained behind, resting at the well's mouth. The woman approaches and Jesus asks for water. She is surprised that Jesus, being a Jew would even speak to her but Jesus then offers her something beyond her ability to comprehend:

John 4:10

10 Jesus answered and said unto her, If thou knewest the gift of God, and who it is that saith to thee, Give me to drink; thou wouldest have asked of him, and he would have given thee living water.

Notice that anytime God asks you for something it is to give you something in return. Jesus asks the woman for something she is not inclined to give, but what happened next made all the difference for her. I ask you what will be your response when the man of

God asks you for something that you are not inclined to give? This woman's life is weighed in the balance by what she does next as will your life be when you are in the same situation with the man or woman of God that He puts in your life.

Jesus offers the woman LIVING WATER. Now, what could this woman conceivably know concerning what Jesus is speaking to her of? She is merely performing a mundane task that she has carried out every day of her life, coming to the well to secure water for the day's needs. In this repetitive, every day task this woman's ability to pay attention to what is really going on will change her life and give her a testimony that stands for 2000 years. Are you personally ready for such an encounter? We often think we have to climb some high mountain or go to a wilderness retreat or a long journey away to hear from God. What we see happening here defies that reasoning. Are you willing to hear from God while you are doing the laundry? I will never forget the day that my wife Kitty was doing the laundry, and the entire property where we were staying was hit by three sharp tremors that only Kitty and I felt. We thought someone had driven a truck or a car into the building, but it was God talking, confirming things that a prophet had warned us would happen just the day before. Are you listening to your prophet? Are you listening to the man or woman of God that He has placed in your life?

Are you willing to hear what the Father would say to you while you are cooking the evening meal, or doing something so basic but at the same time God says that this is your moment? God is always speaking, the question is are we always listening? The woman was alone, and no doubt her thoughts were on matters important to her. Her life was complicated. She had been in six relationships, 5 involving marriage and divorce, and now after being a 5 time loser in love she has lowered the bar and out of convenience and simply not wanting to be alone in life she has willingly placed herself in a common law relationship with a man who didn't love her enough to marry her but was willing to live with her for whatever domestic and conjugal privileges he could illegitimately extract from her in her diminished state. Hers was a joyless existence, to say the least. She no doubt was not held in very high esteem in her community - but God chose to speak to her anyway. God doesn't choose those who think if God is going to say something He is going to tell it to them. He is going to speak to that man or woman or that couple that everyone else has marginalized and written off. Is that you? Then get ready - God is talking to you!

So the woman finds herself coming to this well that was so familiar to her, and she sees Jesus. By his dress and comportment, she recognizes him as a Jew and steels herself against the dispersions that all Samaritan's were familiar with enduring in the presence of those from Judea in the south cast upon those of her village as they traveled through on their way to the Galilee. Contrary to what she expected to happen, Jesus actually engages her as a human being, without insult or pretense. She recoils at first, but Jesus breaks through her hardened exterior and offers her something that constitutes right down to our day the greatest gift that heaven ever proffered to the sons of men. He offered her the gift of Himself as the means by which she might partake of and have activated on the inside of her a resource of life, refreshing and joy that didn't have anything to do with any outward condition or situation. He offered her LIVING WATER predicated on her knowing and recognizing the gift of God.

John 4:10

10 Jesus answered and said unto her, If thou knewest the gift of God, and who it is that saith to thee, Give me to drink; thou wouldest have asked of him, and he would have given thee living water.

WHAT IS THE GIFT OF GOD?

What is the gift of God? As she needed to be able to answer that question, so we need to be able likewise to answer the same. Remember this - knowledge brings release. Knowing the gift of God brings the release of the streams of God on the inside of you. It isn't about learning some convoluted spiritual protocols in prayer to cause heaven's streams to flow in your life. It isn't about being someone you are not or being better than anyone else. It is simply KNOWING the gift of God in the person of Jesus standing before this woman as He stands before us every time the gospel is proclaimed to us. Jesus tells her this insight regarding who He was at that moment made her eligible for what He called LIVING WATER. The word know there implies the act of putting your attention or turning the attentiveness of your mind upon the object in question. What does this mean? You are where your attention takes you. If your focus is on your problems, you are heading into more problems. If your attention is upon Him - upon God, His truth, His glory, His presence you are heading into the gale force release of the streams of heaven in your life that will sweep away all the works of darkness ranged against you.

ACKNOWLEDGING THE GIFT BRINGS THE RELEASE OF GOD'S POWER:

The acknowledgment of the gift of God who is Christ is the predicating revelation that literally opens the whole of the kingdom of God up to you in all its glory and all its power. What is the gift of God? In the previous chapter Jesus met with a leader of the Jews, Nicodemus by name and answered this question with clear clarity:

John 3:16

16 For God so loved the world, that he gave his only begotten Son, that whosoever believeth in him should not perish, but have everlasting life.

This verse is so familiar to us that it's revelatory value is diminished by the commonality of the phraseology. Let us by God's grace look at this verse with virginal eyes, as though we are seeing it for the first time:

For God so loved the world that He gave. This is the most important thing Jesus wants us to know about His Father. He wants us to see Him as a loving God and a giving God. That word love is as you might guess "agapao." It means to love dearly; to be fond of; to be content with. Did you know that God doesn't just love you, He loves you DEARLY. That implies passion and urgency. I love my wife dearly and passionately. From the moment I fell in love with her, I was in hot pursuit and pressing into her life, into

11

a relationship with her no matter what the cost. My whole life became reconstituted and reframed around her life with absolute abandonment. While I hoped that she would return my love and I longed that she would return my love, I was nonetheless enthralled and captivated with her whether she ever returned the same love back to me. That example is just a faint indicator of the kind of love wherewith God loves you. Whether you EVER love Him back this is the love by which He loves you.

Because God loves you, He gives to you. God SO LOVED THE WORLD THAT HE GAVE. Let me tell you something - there are florists across this country whose bank accounts are richer because I so love my wife that I want to give to her. What you love you will give to. When I give to my wife, I don't go out in the backyard and pick a dandelion. I am looking for roses, the sweeter and more numerous the better. When I buy her a piece of jewelry, it is going to cost me something let me tell you. Why? Because I love her. When God loves you, He gives you His best. He scoured heaven's vaults from top to bottom and the only gift that He could provide that would adequately reflect the dimension of His love was the gift of HEAVEN'S DARLING because He loves you, He loves you dearly, He is fond of you, He is contented with you.

What does agapao mean? He is CONTENTED with you. Isn't God always displeased? Doesn't He always have a frown on His ineffable face? I can't find the displeasure of God in John 3:16. Isn't God angry every day? I can't find His anger in John 3:16. Doesn't God thunder His wrath down upon humanity in great outrage? Remember that God's love for you was determined before you ever loved Him and in fact He loved you when you were by nature an enemy of God, shaking your fist in His face. How can we reconcile God's love to man's sinful condition? The answer is that God sees past your sin and loves who He created you to be. The only barrier is, are you going to abandon all obstinacy and self-directed living and pour yourself out like a drink offering to His purposes?

Paul spoke of this love in Ephesians 1:4:

Ephesians 1:4

4 According as he hath chosen us in him before the foundation of the world, that we should be holy and without blame before him in love:

This means that God looked down through time, past the fact that you were born in sin. The sin condition, your sin condition did not give Him pause because of the depth of love wherewith He loves us. He looks past every transgression and all darkness in your life and sees you as something, as someone who was accepted in the beloved, holy and without blame before Him in love before you were ever created - because He was IN LOVE with you. He knew that His ability to love you, with your cooperation would completely obliterate every stain of sin and rebellion in your heart against His lordship. Your faults and failures don't intimidate Him. He loves you because He loves you because He loves you and the only thing that is determinate is whether you by yielding yourself to Him will allow yourself to be the recipient of that love and all that it entails.

This is unconditional love. We've all seen this kind of love. We see a woman or a man love someone and overlook entirely glaring faults, failures and character issues that are absolutely plain to everyone else. Percy Sledge sang a song "When a man loves a woman..." She can do no wrong in his eyes, and even if his best friend speaks against her, His love refuses to see her through any other eyes than that of total approval. This is the love that God loves you with, and because He loves you, He has given to you. Whether you have ever experienced the gift of God or capitalized in life on the gift of God in the past - you must know according to God's word that there is a gift that God has given you of Himself that Jesus describes not only as living water but according to verse 14 it is a spring of water springing up to everlasting life:

John 4:14

14 But whosoever drinketh of the water that I shall give him shall never thirst; but the water that I shall give him shall be in him a well of water springing up into everlasting life.

Because you accept the gift of God you have something EVERLASTING (or irreducible) on the inside of you from God for the intent of blessing you now and always. In other words, this isn't a reservoir of limited capacity but an EVERLASTING (or irreducible) resource on the inside of you as the gift of God's love. It cannot be tapped. It is always available. It is easily accessible. It is at your disposal. It not only quenches thirst, but it also eliminates thirst. What does that mean? It means that the things you need and have need of or desire are spontaneously available on the occasion of your longing as a benefit of the curious nature of the repository of God's Spirit on the inside of you that comes available as you draw upon who He is by faith and who He has made Himself to be on in the depths of your being.

THE SPRINGS, RIVERS, AND POOLS OF GOD'S SPIRIT WITHIN YOU:

If God is something on the inside of us, we ought to know and have a more in-depth understanding of what that is, don't you agree? What is God on the inside of you? He is as water. That word in verse 14 for water describes in the original language:

Water as in springs, rivers, pools or rain. We will come back to rivers in a moment. God is a pool of water on the inside of you. Everybody into the pool! When you have a pool, you want to get in it. A pool by its existence is a standing invitation to dive in. Think about the pool of Bethesda in John 5. The angel came and stirred the waters and the first one in got healed. Why would God do that? He is speaking about something on the inside of you. We cry out for God to heal but we don't understand that healing doesn't come from some OTHERLY elsewhere. Healing occurs when He sends the angel of His presence to stir the waters of your soul and release the healing that has lay resident there on the inside of you - the kingdom of God IN YOU from the creation of the world.

That word water also is the Greek word for rain. Do you realize that the rain of God is not just something outward, but it is something inward that He has placed there by His Spirit? On the inside of you, there is an entire spiritual ecosystem that Jesus called in Luke 17:20, 21 the KINGDOM OF GOD that is WITHIN YOU. We tend to look outwardly for what Jesus is telling this woman would be on the inside of her predicated on putting her attention not on her own troubled life but on the gift of God that He was to her and is to us. What you are looking outwardly in vain for if you will look by the eyes of the Spirit to the inward chambers of your heart where Christ dwells in faith, you will find every resource, every miracle, every answer, every deliverance, every stream of God's goodness bubbling up to life everlasting inviting you to take the plunge and know with fullness and finality the totality of who God is in you and what God is in you and just how deeply He loves you and wants to make Himself known to you.

Turn to John 5:4-8. After talking to the woman at the well about pools, and springs and rain, Jesus makes His way to the pool of Bethesda. Do you think that was by design or by happenstance? There at this pool are a multitude of impotent folk, blind, halt, whithered and waiting for the troubling of the water. The first one in got healed, the others were left in their suffering. The man Jesus speaks to has been there 38 years, doing two things: He was waiting on the troubling of the water, and He was looking for a man. Why was he looking for a man? Because every single person there was looking for a man. They couldn't get in the water, they knew they needed a man to help them. Jesus is standing before this individual and declaring to Him "I am the man that can get you into the waters that will heal you - take up your bed and walk ..." Let me tell you something, you may be waiting for a revival, or waiting for someone with a specific anointing or understanding to finally get you free from your captivity but I am here to declare to you that JESUS in His person on the inside of you is the man you have been looking for all your life. If you will put your attention on HIM and not on some outward person you will experience those dry places on the inside of you to bubble up, flow forth and be your deliverance!

The answer to your need is not in the next book that someone publishes about how to follow some obscure religious principle or protocol in prayer to get your answer. Your deliverance is not in going halfway across the country to get in a meeting where an anointing will be flowing that will set you free. All of those things might be involved, but the reality is that you have a pool of Bethesda on the inside of you right now and right now the angel of God's presence is stirring the waters to activate your faith to provoke you to receive this instant what you have waited for all your life.

Now go to John 6:16-21. Again we see Jesus interacting with His people in the context of water, springs, wells, pools and here on the Sea of Galilee. Jesus sent the disciples into a boat to cross the Galilee. What does that mean to you? Your life is like the Galilee that night, dark, troubled and turbulent. As Jesus put those men on the boat and sent them across, so He has set you in your life and sent you on your way. He told them to cross to the other side, and as a believer in Jesus, you are likewise on a journey across the winds and waves of life at the command of Jesus to get to the other side with your testimony intact. What happened next? A storm blew up. Have you encountered such storms in your day to day existence?

[Jhn 6:21 KJV] 21 Then they willingly received him into the ship: and immediately the ship was at the land whither they went.

Have you ever had a storm blow up in your life? Did you know they name storms? Most of the storms in your life have a name. It could be your husband or your wife's name. It could be your child's name. The phone rings in the middle of the night, and you wake up to answer and find yourself rowing in a gale force wind of emergency room visits, bail bondsmen and court arraignments trying to get your child out of a storm of their own making that you are in the midst of rowing with all your might. We have all faced trials and tribulations of this nature under the command of God to go to the other side. How do we get there? By opening our eyes and seeing Jesus walking on the waters of our soul. When we look at Jesus walking on the waters of our soul and GLADLY RECEIVE HIM into our situation, there will be two things: a great calm and an immediate arrival into your safe harbor.

CONCLUSION:

Jesus is the spring of living water bubbling on the inside of you. Jesus is the pool of Bethesda whose waters the angel of His presence is stirring right now to receive your miracle. Jesus is the one walking toward you on the troubled waves of your inner man to calm you and deliver you and set you free from all captivity. It's all about who He is on the inside of you and not any other thing. God so loved that He gave Jesus. He didn't love us so much He gave us the Christian religion (I don't think that would be very loving). He didn't love us so much He gave us a body of theology (we don't have much appetite for such things). He didn't love us so much He gave us ANY OUTWARD DEPENDENCY - He loved us so much that He gave us Jesus and the only question is, will you receive Him, gladly accept Him into the boat of your life?

CHAPTER TWO

INTRODUCTION

In chapter one we introduced the unique pattern in John chapters 4-7 of Jesus going from one body of water to the next to reveal something of Himself to His disciples and to us by their testimony. We saw when Jesus met the woman at the well that He spoke to her of the gift of God that He is in His person and the promise of SPRINGS OF WATER springing up within you as the outworking of knowing Him as the gift of God. Understand what Jesus means when He says "if you knew the gift of God" is of paramount importance because it contains the predicating promise of springs of water coming forth on the inside of you to everlasting life. Now when we refer to everlasting life, it is more than eternity in heaven, or playing a harp on a fleecy white cloud. It speaks as well to temporal blessing, favor and the dividends of the kingdom in the here and now.

In Jesus' speaking of the gift of God, we are given to understand that it is not something that flows through religious principle or even spiritual principle.

Not everything spiritual is godly, as you may know already. Jesus is in His person the walking manifestation of God's gift to man. We access this gift, and its benefits of living water on the inside of us not by learning principles or gaining "gnosis" or knowledge, but rather through yieldedness and ongoing intimacy with Jesus. The Gift of God is JESUS HIMSELF, made manifest in your life through KNOWING HIM and the Greek word used in John 4:10 means to turn the mind or the attention of your focus upon Him. This is putting your attention on HIM when everything around you is distracting and dismaying you. When you put your attention on Him there promised to us an instantaneous manifestation of divine intervention in your life and your present distress. The perfect example of this is in Numbers 21:8

Numbers 21:8

8 And the Lord said unto Moses, Make thee a fiery serpent, and set it upon a pole: and it shall come to pass, that every one that is bitten, when he looketh upon it, shall live.

The people had been attacked by fiery serpents. There are two kinds of snakes in the Bible, constrictors, and vipers. Constrictors slowly squeeze the life from their victims, but vipers come at you with a blitz attack to put you in a panic and destroy your life and your testimony. Jesus spoke of this in John 3:14:

John 3:14

14 And as Moses lifted up the serpent in the wilderness, even so must the Son of man be lifted up:

The turning of your attention upon Jesus described in John 3:14 is the same thought conveyed in John 4:10 when Jesus spoke of knowing or turning your attention upon Him. When you do this something will start bubbling up on the inside of you that will marginalize and remove every work of darkness against you at that moment. This is not just to be an occasional intervention of heaven but a resident resource on the inside of you flowing out of your riveted focus in every event of your life upon the gift of God who is Jesus, Christ in you the hope of Glory (Col. 1:27). Don't look at the problem so intently that it breaks your focus on who Jesus is and what He is doing in the midst of your challenge.

Colossians 1:27

27 To whom God would make known what is the riches of the glory of this mystery among the Gentiles; which is Christ in you, the hope of glory:

The gift of God Jesus spoke of to the woman at the well is none other than the gift of His indwelling person on the inside of you by virtue of your new birth. Christ in you is the gift of God. Christ in you is the hope of Glory and Phil. 4:9 says that God will meet all your need out of His riches in glory - glory, not in some ephemeral future dimension but here and now on the inside of you - like streams of living water flowing out to arrest your life and transform it according to the parameters set by Jesus "as in heaven, so on earth."

Notice how Jesus describes what happens on the inside of a person who KNOWS (sets his attention on) the gift of God that He is in Himself:

John 4:14

14 But whosoever drinketh of the water that I shall give him shall never thirst; but the water that I shall give him shall be in him a well of water springing up into everlasting life.

When you LOOK upon Him or put your attention on Him in the midst of whatever is taking place in your life - it causes something to flow up out of you called "springs of living water." Now that would be enough. There are probably few believers in the 2000 year history of the church that have entirely taken advantage of what Jesus spoke of concerning Himself in John 4 to the Samaritan woman. But Jesus doesn't stop there. Go to John 5 where we find Jesus visiting another water feature called the pool of Bethesda. He goes to Bethesda and reveals Himself as the one who stirs the water of our soul and heals us by the angel of His presence. There was a man there for 38 years who was looking for an outward stirring, but when Jesus came, he didn't give him something outward but something immediate and inward based on His presence before the man at that moment. He gave Him not an outward stirring but an INWARD STIRRING that would spontaneously produce on the inside of Him what everyone else was waiting for someone or something outwardly to deliver. Ask yourself how many tanks of gas, how many airline tickets, how many conferences, how many countless hours are you going to have to spend before you open your eyes and see Jesus standing before you being in Himself on the inside of you what you have been longing and erroneously seeking to find outwardly that has been inwardly resident in you all along as Christ in you the Hope of Glory?

Let's stop waiting for God to send the angel to stir the church and let Him come and stir our souls and see ourselves spontaneously receive what others don't even realize is available because they are looking outwardly for what God automatically releases to you inwardly when you look upon Him as the impotent man when you know Him like the woman at the well, and what happens? You are in a moment of time forever changed.

Having springs within us as promised in John 4 is lovely. Having the stirring of the angel in our hearts as the man at Bethesda in John 5 is excellent and wonderful - in fact, it will bring your miracle. We don't stop there. Go on to John 6, and we see Jesus engaging His disciples at another water feature called the sea of Galilee. They are rowing in vain against a deadly storm, and Jesus comes walking on the waters of their problem and stepping into their boat. In the moment He gets their attention by walking on the water they experience an instant calm and find themselves in fact suddenly at land! Having Jesus walking on the waters of our adversity to step into our boat and give us a suddenly-at-land experience as in John 6:16-20 is beyond a blessing. But He doesn't leave us there. There is something more. God wants to give us more than the experience of deliverance and blessing. He wants us to have more than crisis intervention or occasional visitation; He wants us to move from VISITATION to HABITATION, from mere springs to ABSOLUTE RIVERS OF HIS POWER not just flowing TO US but ORIGINATING IN US.

OUT OF YOUR BELLY SHALL FLOW RIVERS:

Turn now to John chapter 7. In John 7, we find Jesus in the temple during the Feast of Tabernacles declaring not just a well as in John 4 or a stirring at the pool of Bethesda, or the sudden calming of the storm in the Galilee, but now He turns our attention again to what He is on the inside of us - promising the RIVERS OF GOD to all that believe on Him as the gift of God that He spoke to the Samaritan woman about in John 4:

John 7:37-38

37 -- In the last day, that great day of the feast, Jesus stood and cried, saying, If any man thirst, let him come unto me, and drink. 38 He that believeth on me, as the scripture hath said, out of his belly shall flow rivers of living water.

Notice that He says RIVERS plural out of your BELLY. Why didn't He say out of your heart? The heart speaks of your human spirit, but the belly speaks of something more encompassing:

The Greek word belly here, among other things, describes not just the human spirit but the innermost part of a man, the soul, heart as the seat of thought, feeling choice, or will. In other words, we are talking about God in possession of not just your born again spirit but also your mind, your emotions and your faculty of will just as He is in possession of your human spirit as His habitation through the new birth. In the New Birth, He is in you as springs of LIVING WATER, but as He gains ground in your mind, will and emotions those springs become not just ONE river but many rivers - four in fact. How do we know there are four? Because there are four inner dimensions of man that can be the conduit of His glory and power. They are:

HUMAN SPIRIT

THE EMOTIONS

THE WILL

THE MIND

Now, remember that we are speaking of FOUR dimensions of the ONE river of God on the inside of you (Just as Isaiah 11:1-3 speaks of 7 spirits of God, but we know they are that one and self-same Holy Ghost referred to throughout the New Testament. Jesus promises us RIVERS plural - RIVERS OF GOD FLOWING UP OUT OF US into our lives and the lives of those around us. What was Jesus speaking about? In verse 39 it is made plain, He is talking about your personal Pentecost.

John 7:39

39 (But this spake he of the Spirit, which they that believe on him should receive: for the Holy Ghost was not yet given; because that Jesus was not yet glorified.)

Here Jesus is, standing in the temple, talking about Pentecost on the day of the Feast of Tabernacles. He is trying to tell us what comes next. After Pentecost - what next? After infilling - FULL POSSESSION. After springs and stirrings, rivers of massive power originating in us and through us. After what Ephesians 1 calls the earnest of your inheritance, full manifestation. This is God getting everything that He paid for in the release of Himself through the gift of the cross. This is the total dividend of the cross being paid into your life in complete manifestation in every area of your need.

Now when Jesus said this - speaking of RIVERS of WATER, it is interesting that the Jews start thinking about another body of water:

John 7:40-41

40 Many of the people therefore, when they heard this saying, said, Of a truth this is the Prophet. 41 Others said, This is the Christ. But some said, Shall Christ come out of Galilee?

If you aren't paying attention to the settings where these things take place you are going to miss the more profound truths. We have to look beyond the bonded leather and rice paper and see the living tableau of what is happening here. The Galilee was then and is now the principal source of water for the entire nation of Israel. Without the Galilee, the land of Israel would be as dry as the Levant beyond Mount Nebo. Yet from Jesus' time and before then, the very people whose survival depended on the Galilee, despised its waters just as they despised Jesus. Can any good thing come out of Galilee, was the saying so prevalent at that time and right down to today. Yet if it weren't for the Galilee they would die of thirst, their crops would be blighted and their cities filled with dying children. They despised the very instrument of their salvation. It is interesting to note that June of 2018 the Knesset voted to act in preservation of the Galilee during what is now recognized as a 100-year drought. They have as a legislative body acknowledged that only what comes out of Galilee can save them. First the natural recognition then the spiritual recognition. There are rabbinic scholars who believe that the current drought is a harbinger of the coming of the Messiah - but they still haven't recognized (but soon will) that it was Jesus whom they pierced.

Now when we talk about waters is this just poetic phraseology or are these WATERS or RIVERS

PLURAL specifically? We need to answer this question because what we don't understand we ascribe to poetic language when in fact there is a more profound revelation to be found if we care enough to divine it from God's word. What does the word of God say about RIVERS?

THE LAW OF FIRST MENTION:

There is a law of theological inquiry called the "law of the first mention." It is understood to be that principle by which the first mention of a subject in the Bible becomes a weighted interpretive guide by which that subject can be understood throughout scripture. The first seven mentions of the word river in the scripture are found in the book of Genesis, chapter 2. They refer to the river of God in the midst of the garden of Eden and the four rivers that follow out of that ONE river out of Eden and throughout the surrounding area:

[Gen 2:10-15 KJV] 10 And a river went out of Eden to water the garden; and from thence it was parted, and became into four heads. 11 The name of the first [is] Pison: that [is] it which compasseth the whole land of Havilah, where [there is] gold; 12 And the gold of that land [is] good: there [is] bdellium and the onyx stone. 13 And the name of the second river [is] Gihon: the same [is] it that compasseth the whole land of Ethiopia. 14 And the name of the third river [is] Hiddekel: that [is] it which goeth toward the east of Assyria. And the fourth river [is] Euphrates. 15 And the LORD God took the man, and put him into the garden of Eden to dress it and to keep it.

In Genesis 2 we see God putting man in the garden. There was a river, in fact rivers in that natural location called the Garden of Eden. Through the work of the Cross, God puts the Garden IN YOU, He puts the river of His Spirit in you. When we read the Genesis 2 account, you have to know that God is speaking to you of something that He has put within you by virtue of the New Birth and your subsequent infilling of the Holy Ghost with evidence of speaking in other tongues. There is the one river parting into four rivers constituting five streams. What does the number 5 connote? Five is the number of grace. What is grace? Grace is defined as "the divine influence upon the heart and its reflection in the life." Grace is GOD on the inside of you, changing you and changing the circumstances of your life according to His purpose just as these rivers originated in Eden and flowed out into the earth, some of them even today still giving life and hope to all who come to their banks. This is what God has put on the inside of you. Not just a poetic metaphor, but a living reality. It isn't a metaphor for a river it IS a river as mighty as the Mississippi that dominates this entire nation (the

USA), in fact it is FOUR rivers coming out of the ONE river of God that is the SPIRIT OF GOD on the inside of you, flowing out to four specific aspects of your life encompassing a torrent of grace and power affecting every conceivable area of your need. Let us continue on to study exactly how this fourfold river originating from the one river in the midst of the Garden of God works to transform our lives!

CHAPTER THREE

INTRODUCTION

We are studying the rivers of God spoken of in John 7:37-39. In this passage we see Jesus standing up in the temple at the beginning of what scholars call the year of opposition in His ministry. He stands boldly in the temple during the Feast of Tabernacles and announces Himself as the living fountain, the gift of God in His very own person that IF we partake of, we will never thirst again. What does this mean? We will never thirst again because as a consequence of believing on Him (leaning with our whole heart and personality upon Him with all of our person) there would be then manifest within us not just a river but RIVERS (plural) of living, life-giving, life-altering grace by the infilling of the Holy Spirit to completely change our lives and the lives likewise of those around us as well. Jesus declared it this way:

[Jhn 7:37-39 KJV] 37 In the last day, that great [day] of the feast, Jesus stood and cried, saying, If any man thirst, let him come unto me, and drink. 38 He that believeth on me, as the scripture hath said, out of his belly shall flow rivers of living water. 39 (But this spake he of the Spirit, which they that believe on him should receive: for the Holy Ghost was not yet [given]; because that Jesus was not yet glorified.)

These rivers, Jesus says will flow out of your belly. Your belly is not just your human spirit. The belly in ancient times denoted not only of the spirit of man but the four-fold nature of the inner man including:

1. The Spirit

2. The Emotions

3. The Mind

4. The Will

We all feel the river of God flowing in our Spirit. That is an act of sovereign grace originating in God as He takes up residence within us. However, you need to know that God wants to claim territory and control not only in your Spirit but in your emotions, your will, and your mind. In fact, if this isn't happening in you then you are what Paul describes as a CARNAL CHRISTIAN. You have God in your heart but you haven't given Him access to the rest of your being. Let us be clear: God wants to take territory in your inner man. The inner territory must change before the outer territory reflects the character of "as in heaven so on earth." Because we are carnal and sold under sin, even as professing believers, this causes us to experience unnecessary contradiction to His promise in our lives. His promise is when He has you - ALL OF YOU - inhabiting not only your human spirit but your mind, will and emotional man as well THEN what is a SAMARITAN SPRING (John 4) becomes a mighty FOUR-FOLD river dominating every aspect of your life with God's blessing!

When we read of RIVERS of God we must go to the first mention of RIVERS in the scripture and interestingly enough there is a seven-fold mention of the rivers of God found in the very beginning, in Genesis chapter 2, in the garden of Eden. What is the connotation of the number seven? When God says something seven times what is He getting at? Seven times in three verses God speaks of 5 rivers. One originating river with four tributaries flowing out of the midst of Eden. If that isn't God saying something to you then what is? You have to get this by revelation. You have to look deeper than a precursory, dry consideration of ancient writ. God wants you to see that you have ON THE INSIDE OF YOU an Edenic environment, created by God, guarded by angels, originating something so powerful and fourfold that it can only be described by Jesus not just as a river but RIVERS of everlasting life flowing out of you because you believe in HIM. Why would we want this? Because the rivers maintained the Edenic state in the distant past, likewise the rivers of God's Spirit Jesus speaks of in John 4:37-38 will create and maintain your life in Edenic entitlement (heaven come to earth) as we allow them to dominate us inwardly and flow out through us profusely through the character of our spiritual lives.

The number 5 is the number of grace and in Hebrew, it is spoken of as a pronounced breath "hey". The Spirit of God in both the Old and New Testament language is "ruach" and "pneuma" respectively both meaning as well a "blast or current of air". The five rivers in Eden speak of the RIVER of God's Spirit - the blast of His presence IN YOU flowing OUT OF YOU to impact your life. The Number 7 in Hebrew is "Zayin" and the pictograph of its symbol is a sword. It is the SWORD of the Spirit, the perfection of God on the inside of you by His indwelling Spirit. The number 7 is also called a "crowned vav" because it is drawn by making a number 6 in Hebrew and putting a crown on it - speaking of the authority of the believer in Christ. There are 7 mentions of the word river in Gen. 2:10-14 that is God speaking of what constitutes a WEAPONIZED FLOW of His Spirit on the inside of you to defeat all the works of the enemy. The deliverance you are waiting and praying for is on the inside of you waiting to be unleashed when you open up not just your SPIRIT but the entire BELLY (spirit, mind, will and emotions) in a determinate discipleship to no longer be a carnal being (animated by the flesh) but a spiritual being (animated by the spirit) dominated and disciplined by the Spirit of God on the inside of you to whom you have opened the whole of your inner man in total yieldedness to His mind, will and purpose for you moment by moment and day by day.

HOW DOES THE GARDEN OF EDEN REPRESENT YOUR INNER MAN?

What Adam destroyed by transgression in the garden of Eden (Gen. 3:6), Jesus restored by obedience in the garden of Gethsemane (Luke 22:39-43). It is interesting that the Rabbis in antiquity believed that the Tree of Life was a grapevine. Jesus declares in John 15:1 that He is the vine. He was declaring to the Pharisees and the Scribes that the Tree of Life in the Garden spoken of in their scriptures was none other than Jesus Himself. That which gives life to us is not doctrinal, theological, ecclesiastical, or some spiritual protocol, principle or gnosis. The TREE OF LIFE is a person, and His name is Jesus. When He is in the CENTER of your being then the inner precincts of your being become INWARDLY what the garden of Eden was outwardly in the beginning.

[Gen 2:10-15 KJV] 10 And a river went out of

Eden to water the garden; and from thence it was parted, and became into four heads. 11 The name of the first [is] Pison: that [is] it which compasseth the whole land of Havilah, where [there is] gold; 12 And the gold of that land [is] good: there [is] bdellium and the onyx stone. 13 And the name of the second river [is] Gihon: the same [is] it that compasseth the whole land of Ethiopia. 14 And the name of the third river [is] Hiddekel: that [is] it which goeth toward the east of Assyria. And the fourth river [is] Euphrates. 15 And the LORD God took the man, and put him into the garden of Eden to dress it and to keep it.

Now, God placed a RIVER in the midst of the garden and Jesus said when you believe THAT RIVER will be IN YOU springing up to life everlasting. Now, in Christian culture, we have an innate understanding that there is something called the river of God. We have River Church, River Revival, River this and river that - why is that so compelling to us? Because it is something that is on the inside of us of the Spirit of God that wants to make itself known! Why do you think we call our churches after the RIVER OF GOD? We are *RIVER REVIVAL CHURCH because God is REVIVING THE RIVER! (*This series of messages originally were shared at River Revival church in Sterling, VA). Let us consider the theme of RIVERS in the Scripture:

TURN TO THE BOOK OF REVELATION:

[Rev 22:1 KJV] 1 And he shewed me a pure river of water of life, clear as crystal, proceeding out of the throne of God and of the Lamb.

Humanity commenced in the RIVER of God and concludes moving into eternity future on the banks of the RIVER of God. Natural Eden no longer survives but the River of God in the midst of her still exists today and for you and I and every other believer, it is available according to Jesus in John 7:37-39 as the streams of His Spirit - a mighty torrent capable and available to dominate every aspect of your life to bless and benefit you beyond your expectations.

THE PSALMIST DAVID PUT IT THIS WAY:

[Psa 46:4-6 KJV] 4 [There is] a river, the streams whereof shall make glad the city of God, the holy [place] of the tabernacles of the most High. 5 God [is] in the midst of her; she shall not be moved: God shall help her, [and that] right early. 6 The heathen raged, the kingdoms were moved: he uttered his voice, the earth melted.

David says by the Spirit of Prophecy - there is a river. Where is this river? It is on the inside of you. Not because it is a convenient Christian metaphor, but because Jesus said it was on the Feast of Tabernacles in John 7:37-39. What is the purpose of this river? There is a river, the streams whereof make glad the city of God! This is not the Jordan. Prophetically there will come a time when the Galilee will dry up and the Jordan will be no more but when Jesus comes and His foot touches the Mt. of Olives the mountain will be rent and out of if in fulfillment of scripture will come a river that will transform the land in preparation for the millennial reign of Christ. David was in his palace writing this, on the lower slopes of the Moriah, sensing this in his spirit that though he couldn't see it, all he had was the Gihon spring … he knew that there was a river coming not just a natural river but a SPIRITUAL river that Jesus stands in our temple today to declare just as He stood in that temple in that day declaring to us that if we partake of its waters its streams will make us glad and make glad the city of God. What is the city of God? The writer of Hebrews says it is none other than the church of the living God. What is it that makes us glad as Christians? Ice cream socials? Sunday services? Liturgy, theology or Sunday school lessons? These are all dry husks of dead religion without the RIVER OF GOD flowing on the inside of us.

David says in Psalm 46:5 that the river is special and powerful because GOD is in the MIDST OF HER. This is more than a natural river. It is the Spiritual river Jesus declares to us. Why are we teaching on the river? Because GOD IS IN THE RIVER. He isn't in some far off, inaccessible place. He is IN YOU in the RIVER and (v. 5) the RIVER SHALL NOT BE MOVED because God shall not be moved therefore YOU WILL NOT BE MOVED by the enemy because the river is in you, God is in you and though the heathen rage (v. 6) they will be moved and their kingdoms will be moved but those in whom the river flows will be found to be part of that kingdom that will NEVER BE MOVED because of who He is in the river of His Spirit on the inside of us. Read v. 10:

[Psa 46:10 KJV] 10 Be still, and know that I [am] God: I will be exalted among the heathen, I will be exalted in the earth.

Because of this RIVER of TRUTH regarding who God is on the inside of us we are counseled to BE STILL! If you will still your mind and quiet the outside interference you cannot fail to discern, sense and experience the river of God. Not just THE river but a river that Eden tells us flows out to FOUR HEADS or rivers influencing as we will later see EVERY AREA OF YOUR LIFE.

Be Still for I AM THE RIVER God says.

Be Still and know that I AM THE RIVER in the Midst of You, God says.

Be Still and Know that I AM the River that will be exalted among the heathen and exalted AS THE RIVER THAT IS IN YOU in the earth flows out to dominate and shape your life into the image of as in heaven so on earth. This is what is in you. This is who is in you. The Spirit of God, as a river, dominates the landscape of your life and as a part of God's church dominates the nations of the earth by the power of what flows on the inside of you, that originates in God and brings the nations to heel at the foot of the cross!

WHAT IS TO BE YOUR RESPONSE?

In the book of Ezekiel God revealed the same river that David spoke of. In Ezekiel, we see that it originates under the doors of the temple in heaven that you are. You are the temple and the river is not just in you - it is flowing out from you:

[Eze 47:1, 3-9 KJV] 1 Afterward he brought me again unto the door of the house; and, behold, waters issued out from under the threshold of the house eastward: for the forefront of the house [stood toward] the east, and the waters came down from under from the right side of the house, at the south [side] of the altar. ... 3 And when the man that had the line in his hand went forth eastward, he measured a thousand cubits, and he brought me through the waters; the waters [were] to the ankles. 4 Again he measured a thousand, and brought me through the waters; the waters [were] to the knees. Again he measured a thousand, and brought me through; the waters [were] to the loins. 5 Afterward he measured a thousand; [and it was] a river that I could not pass over: for the waters were risen, waters to swim in, a river that could not be passed over. 6 And he said unto me, Son of man, hast thou seen [this]? Then he brought me, and caused me to return to the brink of the river. 7 Now when I had returned, behold, at the bank of the river [were] very many trees on the one side and on the other. 8 Then said he unto me, These waters issue out toward the east country, and go down into the desert, and go into the sea: [which being] brought forth into the sea, the waters shall be healed. 9 And it shall come to pass, [that] everything that liveth, which moveth, whithersoever the rivers shall come, shall live: and there shall be a very great multitude of fish, because these waters shall come thither: for they shall be healed; and everything shall live whither the river cometh.

What are we to do with the river of God in us? We are to plunge in. Not just a nodding commitment of accepting Jesus into our heart. We are to diligently in an applicational way find out with all our capacity to learn and implement how to abandon ourselves not just in our human spirit in the new birth but in every aspect of our being MIND, WILL, AND EMOTIONS how to open the dry chambers of our soul to the rushing currents of that mighty river of God that is on the inside of you. Not just a spring. Not just a well. But a river - cleansing you, changing you and coming out of you where there are waters to swim in where the fish (lost souls) are abundant and the fruits of God are made utterly made manifest.

When the waters come out from the temple that YOU ARE, they flow out into your life, relationships, supply, etc., and everywhere they flow there will be FISH (we are fishers of men, souls of men) and there will be life where the RIVER(S) plural flow. What are the RIVER(S) plural? This is more than poetry this is a revelational truth. We will discover the four rivers, what their names are and what their purposes are in the remainder of this series of teachings.

CHAPTER FOUR

INTRODUCTION

In John 7:37-39 Jesus declares that believing In Him will cause RIVERS of living water to flow out of our belly:

[Jhn 7:37-39 KJV] 37 In the last day, that great [day] of the feast, Jesus stood and cried, saying, If any man thirst, let him come unto me, and drink. 38 He that believeth on me, as the scripture hath said, out of his belly shall flow rivers of living water. 39 (But this spake he of the Spirit, which they that believe on him should receive: for the Holy Ghost was not yet [given]; because that Jesus was not yet glorified.)

We have implied that this statement by Jesus is more than poetic expression but is, in fact, exact language descriptive of the reality of the indwelling of the Holy Ghost in the life of one who BELIEVES in Jesus. Now the word believe means many things to us and even in scripture, there are different words used to define "belief" in Jesus. The specific word in John 7:38 carries the meaning "to put your attention on…" It could not be simpler. Do not be distracted from taking your eyes off of Jesus, whatever is going on in your situation. The word picture would include the image of Moses lifting up the serpent in the wilderness and saying "look and live" as recorded in Numbers 21:8-9. The people were facing attack and certain death from fiery serpents, but those that tore their eyes away from the hissing snakes at their feet about to strike were those who lived and all others perished in torment and agony. Likewise, when we are in agony and facing terror-filled circumstances we are to put our attention upon Him. Why? Because you are where your attention takes you. If you can't take your eyes off the problem, you are headed into more problems. If you look to Him - then you will experience being seated with Him in heavenly places and suddenly out of your middle - out of your belly will flow RIVERS OF LIVING WATER.

What are these RIVERS? Again, they are more than a poetic metaphor. God spoke to me once saying "it isn't a metaphor for a river - it is a river…" I have lived my whole life near the mighty Mississippi and it is one of the great untamed waterways of the earth. The Core of Engineers has worked and our government has spent billions of dollars over the course of decades but the river continually breaks out, establishing its dominance over the land. That is the magnitude of what God has placed on the inside of you. How can the enemy withstand what is coming out of you when it is the RIVER OF GOD? This is what Isaiah spoke of:

[Isa 59:19 KJV] 19 So shall they fear the name of the LORD from the west, and his glory from the rising of the sun. When the enemy shall come in like a flood, the Spirit of the LORD shall lift up a standard against him.

What is the flood? The flood is not the enemy, the flood comes from the river and the river(s) is in you! These are the RIVERS OF GOD flowing out of you raising a standard - a tsunami of God's power to overwhelm every frontal assault of the enemy against you. It doesn't come from above, it comes from within. It is more than a singularity, it is RIVERS plural. What are those RIVERS? We can read John 7:37-39 and inquire about the RIVERS by looking for the first mention of RIVERS in the scripture. We don't have to look far. In Genesis 2 we find the first mention of rivers actually repeated 7 times. When God says something 7 times we need to pay attention. 7 is God's number of perfection. The 5-fold ministry in Eph. 4:11-12 is here to perfect the saints. If 7 is the number of perfection then it is in our best interest to pay attention to the 7's we find in scripture. At the beginning before the fall we find two mentions of 7's, seven days and seven mentions of rivers. The seven days speak of God's process AROUND US. The seven mentions of rivers speak of God's power flowing through us:

[Gen 2:10-15 KJV] 10 And a river went out of Eden to water the garden; and from thence it was parted, and became into four heads. 11 The name of the first [is] Pison: that [is] it which compasseth the whole land of Havilah, where [there is] gold; 12 And the gold of that land [is] good: there [is] bdellium and the onyx stone. 13 And the name of the second river [is] Gihon: the same [is] it that compasseth the whole land of Ethiopia. 14 And the name of the third river [is] Hiddekel: that [is] it which goeth toward the east of Assyria. And the fourth river [is] Euphrates. 15 And the LORD God took the man, and put him into the garden of Eden to dress it and to keep it.

Now we see a river flowing out of Eden and dividing into four heads or tributaries. What is Eden? Does it mean anything more to us other than what is now a bleak landscape in central Iraq with a few straggly goats and shacks on it? The indicator is in reference to the tree of Life in the midst of the garden. In antiquity, Rabbinical sources believed that the Tree of Life was a grapevine. What does that remind you of? In John 15:1 Jesus declared that He is the vine. What is He saying? His listeners, particularly the scribes and Pharisees knew exactly what He was saying. He was saying "I am the tree of life in the midst of your garden…" The Jews believed they were God's garden as a nation. They read Isaiah and believed that they were the only garden that God was interested in. We know however that God wants more than to dwell in the midst of a nation He wants to dwell in your midst in your very person as His temple, planting the Tree of Life in your heart as He put the same tree of Life in the garden before the fall. The garden of God, the Eden of God speaks then of where the Tree of Life that is Jesus is found and He is found in YOU. The Tree of Life is in You and Jesus says that there are RIVERS plural found in you, flowing out of the ONE RIVER and encompassing all of your life as the four tributaries of that one river that came out of Eden encompassed all the land about it and even as some of those rivers still do in the Levant on the Arabian peninsula today.

GETTING THE RIVERS ACTIVATED IN YOU:

Gen. 2:10 tells us that out of Eden came a river dividing itself into four tributaries or secondary rivers. Likewise according to Jesus in John 7:37-39 out of YOU is intended to come a river, in fact, rivers. How do you know the rivers are coming out of you? When the enemy can't stand before you. If the enemy can successfully resist you then the rivers haven't been activated yet. How do we activate them? Jesus said in

51

John 7 the rivers are activated by BELIEVING in Him. Believing on Him by putting your attention on Him in the midst of your pressure. You are where your attention takes you. Paul put it this way in Col. 3:

[Col 3:1-2 KJV] 1 If ye then be risen with Christ, seek those things which are above, where Christ sitteth on the right hand of God. 2 Set your affection on things above, not on things on the earth.

Notice verse 2 of Col. 3. We are to "SET OUR AFFECTION" that word affection is interesting and we don't exactly have an English word that rightly expresses it. It means we are to set our emotional attenuation upon Christ. That means you choose by an act of your will not to be affected or moved emotionally by what is going on around us because our emotional attenuation in the midst of our pressure is not on the source of our pressure producing stress but upon CHRIST WHO SITS ON THE THRONE OF OUR LIFE. How does that look? It's like this - pressure comes, and the storm comes in life and your response is "Jesus! You've got mail!" Then you look to Him as Moses lifted up the serpent and the people looked and lived. You commanded to LOOK (put your attention on Jesus and not the problem) AND LIVE. How does that work? You LOOK to Him and as you look something begins to stir on the inside of you that produces the enemy's downfall and your deliverance. You look and as the angel troubled the water at Bethesda you are the FIRST one in because the waters aren't OUT THERE SOMEWHERE they are IN YOU, in fact, ORIGINATING IN YOU to deliver you and destroy all the works of the devil against you.

Your inner man is the garden of God. Your inner man is your Eden. Because you have accepted the blood of Christ as your salvation, the angels are no longer barring your access to the tree of Life that Jesus is. Eden means "pleasure" or "delightsome". That is the banner over your life that God intends. Is that the banner over your life? When others look at you what is the banner that they see? Or do they see something else? Is the banner over you:

STRESSED OUT!
I'M TIRED!
FED UP!
BURNED OUT!
WORRIED!
FEARFUL!
SICK AND TIRED OF BEING SICK AND
TIRED!
DISTRACTED!
POLLUTED!
SIN-SICK!

What is the banner over your life? God says that the banner He wants to apply to your life is DELIGHTSOME! PLEASURABLE! Jesus put it this way:

[Luk 12:32 KJV] 32 Fear not, little flock; for it is your Father's good pleasure to give you the kingdom.

What is the kingdom? It is IN YOU. It is the RIVERS (plural rivers) of GOD FLOWING OUT OF YOU to dominate the landscape of your life in every area of your life. Your human spirit is the garden of God and Jesus is the tree of Life in the midst of your garden. He is the tree of Life and in because He is in you then originating in you according to v. 10 is a river SINGULAR that flows out in four aspects out into the landscape of your life beyond the precincts of your human spirit. What is the river? It is the one that David spoke of:

[Psa 46:4 KJV] 4 [There is] a river, the streams whereof shall make glad the city of God, the holy [place] of the tabernacles of the highest.

It is the one Ezekiel spoke of as flowing out of the house of the Lord - the restoration Temple that you are in Your Person:

[Eze 47:1 KJV] 1 Afterward he brought me again unto the door of the house; and, behold, waters issued out from under the threshold of the house eastward: for the forefront of the house [stood toward] the east, and the waters came down from under from the right side of the house, at the south [side] of the altar.

It is the river John the Revelator spoke of in Rev. 22:

[Rev 22:1-2 KJV] 1 And he shewed me a pure river of water of life, clear as crystal, proceeding out of the throne of God and of the Lamb. 2 In the midst of the street of it, and on either side of the river, [was there] the tree of life, which bare twelve [manner of] fruits, [and] yielded her fruit every month: and the leaves of the tree [were] for the healing of the nations.

Is this just in heaven? Does not the throne of God exist in us? Wherever the throne of God is present the river is present, the tree of life is present and the glory is present. What will be evident to every eye and confessed by every tongue (one day eventually) is a reality IN YOU - in the GLORY NOW at the present time. You have in you now an "as in heaven so on earth" reality in your called the river of God needing and wanting to be released. You know this is true. You may not be able to articulate it but you know there is something flowing in you that originates in God. It may just be a well but it is intended to be a river. It may be a river but it is intended to be a four-fold something not just in you but flowing out of you to dominate the landscape of your life in every aspect.

How do we get the living waters in us to become a river? By letting it flow as John 7:37-39 state - not just out of our heart as a well of living water springing up to refresh us, but to dominate your whole man referred to as the BELLY. The river of God will NEVER DOMINATE THE CIRCUMSTANCES OF YOUR LIFE until it inundates and dominates the INNER GEOGRAPHY of your entire SOUL, MIND, WILL, AND EMOTIONS. How does that happen? By believing - looking to Jesus, focusing our emotional attenuation upon Him in the midst of the rigors of life even when the fiery serpents of the sudden assault of the enemy come against us. When we take that stand then suddenly that water cooler of spiritual refreshment begins to shake and quake and erupt into a mighty fourfold river that will not be denied but will obliterate all the works of the enemy against us FROM WITHIN US from within CHRIST IN YOU THE HOPE OF GLORY.

It isn't just a singular river we see in Gen. 2:10-14, it is a four-fold river dividing from four heads. There is HEADSHIP in the river. We don't like headship in our culture. We want to submit to no one. Jesus said in Matt 4:19 "follow Me and I will make you…" and there is something in us that rebels against that. Let me tell you something - when a river flows it takes charge everywhere it goes. You are the landscape that the river of God must dominate you inwardly before your circumstances will ever yield outwardly. If your circumstance isn't changing - check your heart. Four is the number "daleth" meaning the door. We say we have opened the door of our heart but that door is a four-fold something including your SPIRIT, MIND, WILL, AND EMOTIONS. He said He will come in and sup but we wonder why we aren't supping? Why are we filling our famished soul with worldly things? Because we have opened our spirits up to receive the New birth but our soul, our mind, will, and emotions are still dabbling and satiating themselves with the pleasures of the world.

THE RIVER PISON through the land of HAVILAH (Have-a-Lot) WHERE THERE IS GOLD:

There is among the four rivers of God a river dedicated just to the acquisition of supply and the transfer of the wealth. In Gen. 2:10-14 these rivers are all spoken of as ENCOMPASSING the lands they flow through. That means that the river cuts off everything else. The rivers of God in you will cause you to walk in separation. They will separate you from sin but they will also separate you from lack, sickness, death itself. You may see bad things happening or threatening beyond the flow of God in your life but you refuse to leave the place of abiding in Him to go and partake of THAT that the world has to offer because you know if you cross that line you are walking into a waste howling wilderness where the river will not refresh you!

The Rivers are RIVER(S) plural. Verse 11 tells us that the name of the first river is PISON and it compasses the land of HAVILAH where there is GOLD. Interesting that this is the first river. John said:

[3Jo 1:2 KJV] 2 Beloved, I wish above all things that thou mayest prosper and be in health, even as thy soul prospereth.

In the gospels before Jesus ever preached or taught, He would address health issues and creature comforts. Healing it has been said is the dinner bell to salvation. The first river that gets activated in your life is the one that goes out into the landscape of life around you and gets the gold and brings it back into your Eden. It compasses the land of Havilah. I like to call it the land of Have-a-lot. God is not a God of poverty. There is something flowing out of you that goes out and gets the gold of God to produce what John 10:10 calls life and life more abundantly. 2 Cor. 8:9 says that Jesus became poor so that we could be rich. If you aren't rich then you haven't received everything that God has for you. Some say this is spiritual riches but the context of 2 Cor. 8:9 for 3 chapters is natural provision. There is a river of God in you that once released will produce supply - abundant supply in your life.

How about a confirmation? Pison means "increase". The increase of God is a river on the inside of you. How does it get released? By putting your attention or your emotional attenuation not upon the financial challenge in our life but upon who God is in your life. It is about making Him Lord over what little increase you have and He takes it and turns it from a trickle into a mighty torrent of supply and provision. There is an INCREASE in you. It is a part of the RIVER of God coming out of the temple of your human spirit. You see the river is ONE river in your spirit but when it flows out of your spirit it becomes a four-fold force or river of the Spirit of God and one whole aspect of it is focused upon supply, the gold of God in your life.

The river of God's increase flows out of you into something very familiar to you whether you realize it or not. It flows in your life already and is connotated by where this river of the increase of God flows. The Pison flows through the land of Havilah. Now what does Havilah mean and what does it infer in your life? The word Havilah means "circle" or "cyclical". Is there anything cyclical in your life? If you live on planet earth regardless of how your finances accrue to you they are CYCLICAL IN NATURE. Paychecks are paid on a cyclical schedule - TGIF! Dividends of investments are paid on a cyclical schedule. Even if you are on a fixed income you receive your support check or annuity check on a cyclical schedule. Likewise, all your bills and expenditures, for the most part, are cyclical in the demand they make upon you every week, every month and every year at tax time. The cyclical nature of supply and demand has given birth to sayings like:

What goes around comes around.

Payday doesn't come every Friday but it does come.

What you reap - so shall you sow.

What is this in terms of the geography of your life? It is the land of Havilah or the cyclical topography of life that controls supply and demand in your day to day existence. God has a river called the river of increase that is ordained to come out of the TEMPLE that you are and encompass or take dominion over these cycles of supply and demand, increase and expenditure in your life and in this land whether you know it or not there is GOLD which is the universal symbol for increase and supply and provision and has been since the dawn of time. Do you get this? There is a RIVER of God, one of the FOUR rivers originating from the ONE RIVER OF GOD'S SPIRIT (a total of 5), arising in your human spirit that is specifically designed to bring INCREASE - to go out into that cyclical circumstance and situation of the day to day grind and bring back the GOLD OF GOD - what some have called the TRANSFER OF THE WEALTH originating in you and being brought inexorably to you because you are BELIEVING on Him as Jesus said in John 7:37-38 - not looking at the supply or the lack of supply but turning your face toward Him - seeking His face FINANCIALLY and seeing His hand providentially in your life.

Now, if this is so, why isn't it working in your life? Remember that it says OUT OF YOUR BELLY. You have it in your heart to be blessed financially. You know in your heart - your human spirit you have MOUNTAIN MOVING FAITH. You know that you have MILLION DOLLAR FAITH on the inside of you. You have it in your heart to give. But that isn't enough. We have to get what is in your heart out into your life. If that is going to happen what is in your heart has to get past your MIND, your WILL, and your EMOTIONS. Otherwise, you have mountain moving faith yet you are being held back by a mere molehill of unbelief and failure to act the enemy inspires against you by provoking to look at circumstances rather than Christ (look at live!). The BELLY Jesus speaks of is not just your HEART or

HUMAN SPIRIT, in ancient times the BELLY was an all-encompassing term defining yes, yes your human spirit but also your mind, will and emotions. How does that work regarding the river of increase that Jesus says will come out of you? Consider the following:

Your Emotions:

[2Co 9:7 KJV] 7 Every man according as he purposeth in his heart, [so let him give]; not grudgingly, or of necessity: for God loveth a cheerful giver.

You have to get your emotions aligned with what is in your Spirit man.

Your Will:

[Exo 35:5 KJV] 5 Take ye from among you an offering unto the LORD: whosoever [is] of a willing heart, let him bring it, an offering of the LORD; gold, and silver, and brass,

You have to get your WILL aligned with what is in your heart regarding finances.

Your Mind:

The Dictionary describes mindfulness in a couple of ways, with the first being, "The state or quality of being mindful or aware of something."

[1Jo 3:17 KJV] 17 But whoso hath this world's good, and seeth his brother have need, and shutteth up his bowels [of compassion] from him, how dwelleth the love of God in him?

Faith works by love. John 3:16 - for God so loved that He gave. God's love in your first and foremost will make you a giver and an investor in the kingdom by giving into the anointing and giving into the needs of those around you.

[Act 4:34-35 KJV] 34 Neither was there any among them that lacked: for as many as were possessors of lands or houses sold them, and brought the prices of the things that were sold, 35 And laid [them] down at the apostles' feet: and distribution was made unto every man according as he had need.

Hebrews 11:1 says that faith is the substance of things hoped for and James 2:17 says faith without works is dead. How does that work in the area of finances? What you have faith to GIVE is a measurement of what you have faith to receive. Matt. 19:29 and Matt. 10:30 teach us to believe for the 100 fold return. What is a hundredfold return on what you give? If you calculate that formula based on your actual giving, you have located yourself. What you have faith to give - what you actually have to give and are following through in actually giving is an exact metric of what you have faith to receive. If you have faith to give $10,000 you have faith to receive a million dollars. You know you have a million dollars in you but you have to get your mind, will and emotions aligned with that for that dimension of faith to cause that money to be made manifest in your life. How does that happen? By filling your MIND with thoughts of giving $10,000. By getting your emotions engaged and getting giddy and cheerful about giving $10,000. By getting your will involve and giving what you can toward that goal until the day you find yourself in reality GIVING $10K and THEN and ONLY THEN does the river of increase BURST out of your inner man, out of the temple that you are and encompass that cyclical landscape of supply and demand in your life to CREATE the 100 fold return of exactly what you have activated by your engagement and cooperation with God's promise. You won't do it if you don't believe it. If you do believe it your pressing in doing what you can, giving what you can toward that goal. If you aren't doing it it is because you aren't believing it. You may believe it in your human spirit but your mind will and emotions have to get engaged and brought into cooperation and THEN the transfer of the wealth of God with your name on it will find you and fund you and transform your life in the financial arena. Is that the end of the matter? No, there are THREE OTHER IMPORTANT RIVERS TO CONSIDER in our ongoing messages in the remainder of this series.

CHAPTER FIVE

INTRODUCTION

In John 7:37-39 Jesus declares that the well of living water that He declared to the woman at the well in John 4:14 can and will become a river, in face RIVER(S) plural out of our belly. The belly refers to more than just your heart or human spirit. When Jesus dwells in your heart by faith, there comes into your human spirit a residency of the presence of God that functions like a well of refreshing you can draw on that will bless your life and hold you fast in Christ. This well is not just a blessing for you it is also a responsibility you bear. When we say you are responsible that implies you are accountable and have authority in God to carry out that duty of ruling and reigning in Him. In fact, you are scripture declares a KING and a PRIEST as well in God.

Rev. 1:6 and Rev. 5:10 declare that you are a king and a priest unto God. In ancient times every place where a well was found, a priest was appointed. Remember, that Moses' father-in-law Jethro was a priest of the wells at Midian (Ex. 18:1). You likewise are a priest over the well that God has placed on the inside of you. Your priesthood in Christ is not just a general sense of ministry but a specific responsibility to superintend AND dispense of the waters of God's Spirit placed in you by the New Birth. This doesn't stop just with the New Birth and making sure you are on your way to heaven after you die. The well in you is intended to become a river resourcing you as well in the here and now. Isn't it interesting that in Ezekiel 47 that the entire temple of God is sitting on a river that then flows out from the altar into the whole earth? You then are a priest of the well and a priest of the river of God intended to flow freely in your life. It is astounding that for 2000 years men have taught on the priesthood of God and the priesthood of the believer but no one has made this connection what this teaching is referring to from the plain testimony of God's word. You are the priest of the well of God IN YOU and you are a priest of a river of God IN YOU and flowing out of you, in fact, you are the temple of God because of that well and because of that river.

The river that God has placed in you is not a singular something but Jesus says that they are RIVER(S) plural. That is more than poetic expression. When Jesus said things the disciples didn't understand they didn't conclude that they lacked understanding, they simply concluded that

Jesus was being spiritual, or speaking a parable. That is the pride of man not wanting to admit there is something in God that has eluded their comprehension. The reference to rivers is Jesus speaking with specificity toward that which is plainly referred to in Gen. 2:10-14.

In Eden, (which represents your person as the dwelling place of God), there is the Tree of Life that the Rabbis believed was a grapevine. Jesus knew this and declared in John 15:1 that He was the vine and we are the branches. He is the river and we are the tributaries. He is the river and the river is in us AS us! He is the river in you and out of the river in Eden came four tributaries or rivers. We elaborated on the first one in the last teaching. These four rivers are:

The Pison

The Gihon

The Hiddekel

The Euphrates

Now Pison means "river of increase". It flows into the land of Havilah where there is gold, bdellium, and the onyx stone. Havilah means "circular". Have you done time in Havilah, going around in circles like you aren't going anywhere? You will notice in Gen. 2:11 that the Pison (God's river bringing the increase in your life) is described as ENCOMPASSING or taking authority over the land of Havilah (circular experiences in life). Do you see the picture that God is giving you? This circular nature of the nature of supply has a spiritual, not just a natural origination. This is what Ezekiel saw on the plain in Chebar. This is God's WHEEL within a WHEEL. The wheel of God's river of increase encompassing and taking authority over the circular nature of life that has bearing specifically on the gold of God being accrued into your situation as supply, provision, and increase.

It is important to know that there is not just gold but also according to v. 12 of Gen. 2 "bdellium and onyx stone". These speak of something God wants you to be infused with when you are feeling like you are going in circles not getting anywhere. Bdellium is a resin that is secreted by a tree and is of great value. In the scriptures, believers are referred to as trees. You are a tree of God and when you are feeling as though you are going in circles in life - something will be excreted from you? Is it fragrant and valuable or is it something else? Another thing about bdellium is when the sunlight shines on it - it liquifies. This speaks of the influence of the Spirit of God on your life when you feel like you are going in circles. When God tries to reach you in that place do you harden your heart or do you simply melt in compliance to what He is telling you? Your pastor knows. When you are in the circular place and your pastor is trying to point the way are you cooperative or do you shine him on, marginalizing his wisdom? When it comes to giving or a giving opportunity does your heart melt or harden when the ushers come to the front with the offering envelopes?

The other valuable thing you will find in this wheel within the wheel of the Pison encompassing the land of Havilah on the inside of you is onyx. Onyx in ancient times represented courage. When soldiers would go into battle knowing they would spend the entire day hacking away at the bodies of their enemies in desperate hand to hand combat, they would carry onyx stones with them because they believed it gave them courage. The river of increase will bring you then pliability to the light of God in your life and courage to obey in all things. Then the gold will be made manifest and not until. You must be yielded and courageous within to see the abundance and supply without that God has for you in Havilah, the cyclical nature of supply and demand, increase and expenditure in your life.

We often ask the question "where is all the money… why am I not experiencing increase as God promised…" but we aren't cooperating with the wheel-within-the-wheel process that comes as God's river of the increase comes out of us to dominate the landscape of our life. We must be pliable. We must have courage. Then the gold of God, the transfer of the wealth of God into your life will be capitalized into your experience.

There are three more rivers to consider. They all flow from that one river of God flowing out from under the temple of God that you are. Do you know the River of God is in you? You know that it is. You know that it is by the witness of the Spirit that tells you that you are born again and Christ dwells in your heart by faith. What you need to understand is that river in you is for the purpose of doing more than registering the warmth of God's presence in your heart. There must come a release. The river in your human spirit of God's glory on the inside of you must be allowed to flow to all your belly (MIND, WILL, AND EMOTIONS) before it will ever flow into your life and change things that seem like they will never change. The inner territory must become the floodplain of God's Spirit before the outer geography of your life, relationships, health, and finances benefit from what comes out of that river of God. Until you yield in your mind, will and emotions all you have is a well to get you by till Jesus comes. God wants you to have MORE than that. When your inner territory is conquered by the ONE river of God on your spirit then it will become FOUR RIVERS flowing out to dominate your life with His goodness. The first is the

71

Pison affecting your natural supply and blessing. When the first river dominates you inwardly and flows into your life outwardly the blessings of Abraham will manifest. It will be said of you what was said of Abraham that he was rich - very rich in all the things necessary for your life.

THE SECOND RIVER OF GOD - THE GIHON

Then we come to the Gihon. The Gihon speaks of something that comes out of you to encompass (take authority over and master) the darkness in your life. The Gihon encompassed (took authority over) the land of Ethiopia. Ethiopia in Hebrew means "land of darkness". Are you dealing with darkness, the darkness of the enemy in your life? Is there darkness in your children that you can't pay off of them? Are you experiencing dark times in your marriage or other areas of your life? God put a resource inside of you that is prefigured by what He describes in Genesis 2 in a seven-fold reference to His rivers IN YOU that Jesus promises us concerning in John 7:37-39. There is something God intends to flow in you that will come out of you and address the darkness in your life! You don't have to just put up with it. It is not correct to wallow in darkness, cringing and waiting for God to do something. He put His river in you as He put the staff in Moses' hand asking him "what is that in thy hand Moses?" You have in God on the inside of you what is necessary to defeat the darkness if you just know and will be obedient to release that river to dominate all areas of darkness coming against you.

What overcomes darkness? Do you lay siege to it in prayer? Do you war against it with your faith? If you understand what the name "Gihon" means you will get a clear strategy for dealing with the darkness of the enemy coming against you. Gihon means "bursting forth". We could say this is the BREAKTHROUGH RIVER. It carries the same meaning as the word "prosper" found in 2 Chron. 20:20 that says "believe the prophets so shall you prosper..." Do you believe the prophets? Who is the prophet in your life? The word believe the prophets so shall you PROSPER means "so shall you COME TO BREAKTHROUGH ..." or as Gen. 2:13 suggests to us - so shall you burst through all the darkness that is trying to range itself against your life. The prophet isn't the breakthrough but the words of the prophet and the leadership of the prophetic in your life will bring you to breakthrough and cause you to burst forth out of the darkness coming against you if you act on it and follow the counsel of the prophets God has placed in your life.

What a testimony of God. The one river of God bringing forth a fourfold blessing in your life. And the first two are all about INCREASE (Pison) and

73

BREAKTHROUGH (bursting-forth Gihon) out of the going in circles experience and out of the darkness that the enemy is trying, always trying to encroach upon your life and your family with. This is the Spirit of Counsel that Isa. 11:1-2 speaks of that will put you over in your situation if you receive it and act upon it in faith with consistent commitment, stepping out with resolute determination that you are going to have all that God has promised you in His word and by the prophets.

CHAPTER SIX

INTRODUCTION

The previous chapters delineate for us that the well of living water (John 4:14) that is in us at salvation is intended by God to become a river, in fact, RIVER(S) plural on the inside of us (John 7:37-39). This increase of the Spirit of God on the inside of us takes place as the dominion of the Spirit of God in the dwelling place of our human spirit breaks out and takes possession of our mind, will and emotions in a causative way that reflects in our character the attributes that make God - God. Paul called this (Eph. 1:13-14) the redemption of the purchased possession. This is God getting what He paid for in your life and your life consequently taking on His character, power, and glory. This is what the apostle Paul referred to in Phil. 3:13 as "being apprehended" by God, and in Rom. 8:19 as the manifestation of the sons of God. God wants and desires to see your mind, will and emotions to manifest outwardly what His inward possession of your human spirit constitutes as His residence, His temple, and place on indwelling in you in the earth on this side of heaven.

When the temple that you are begins to enlarge itself in your life then Ez. 47:1-5 says that there will be a river of God flowing out of you throughout the geography of your life creating a floodplain of God's power and grace that will give you what Ezekiel saw to be waters to swim in. Now make no mistake - in your life, there are waters to swim in whether they are the waters of God or not. Leviathan, who in Job 41 is identified as the king of all the children of pride, he swims in the waters of your unsanctified humanity in every place and in every point that the influence of God has not overwhelmed and taken possession of your mind, will, and emotions. What are the characteristics of Leviathan? Job 41 describes this spirit of pride as:

[Job 41:15-16 KJV] 15 [His] scales [are his] pride, shut up together [as with] a close seal. 16 One is so near to another, that no air can come between them.

What does this mean? Being so opinionated, so full of our own thoughts that like the scales of a sea serpent, no air (or pneuma - spirit) can get past them into your inner man. How many times do we take the posture with God "God I just don't understand what you are doing and saying…" and then we just get stuck there for years of our life because we have allowed pridefulness of mind to be the gatekeeper of our yieldedness to God? We might even weep and cry "if I only understood what God's plan was I would move forward..." This too is pride. It is Leviathan swimming in the waters of sinful human nature. What is the answer? Solomon called it "praying toward the Holy Temple" not in Jerusalem, but on the inside of you - looking to the waters of God that are seeking to come forth out of your temple, not as just a trickle or a spring but a mighty river going out to dominate the entire landscape of your life.

That river of God that comes out of you according to John 7:37-39 becomes a fourfold tributary that is revealed in Genesis 2:10-14:

[Gen 2:10-14 KJV] 10 And a river went out of Eden to water the garden; and from thence it was parted, and became into four heads. 11 The name of the first [is] Pison: that [is] it which compasseth the whole land of Havilah, where [there is] gold; 12 And the gold of that land [is] good: there [is] bdellium and the onyx stone. 13 And the name of the second river [is] Gihon: the same [is] it that compasseth the whole land of Ethiopia. 14 And the name of the third river [is] Hiddekel: that [is] it which goeth toward the east of Assyria. And the fourth river [is] Euphrates.

Your inner man is the garden of God. We know this because Jesus is the Tree of Life. The Rabbi's believed in antiquity that this tree was a grapevine

78

and Jesus says in John 15 that we are to abide in the vine that He is. Out of this Eden, out of your human spirit comes a river that manifests in four variations:

THE PISON (RIVER OF INCREASE):

That encompasses Havilah (the cycles of life) to bring forth the gold of God, provision, and supply in your life.

THE GIHON (RIVER OF BREAKTHROUGH, OR BURSTING FORTH):

That dispels the encroachment of the enemy and the darkness of the enemy against you. Breakthrough is not some random intervention of God in your life. Breakthrough, or bursting forth out of darkness is a resource, a flow a current, a mighty river that God has put on the inside of you that is deployable and can be activated IN YOU in the glory to overcome every obstacle in your life. Say this to yourself: "the breakthrough is IN ME…" If you can receive it, in Christ you ARE the breakthrough. That is why when Moses was saying "stand still and see the salvation of God, that the Father rebuked him, asking "what is that in your hand…" The breakthrough you are waiting for from on high is IN YOU in the glory and will spontaneously manifest in your life for victory and deliverance as you allow it to deal with the Ethiopia -

the darkness on the inside of you - then the darkness around you will be utterly dispelled. There is no outward victory without successful, inward conquest.

So we see that the river of God on the inside of you is a river of increase, a river of breaking forth and the third river, the Hiddekel is now to be addressed:

Gen. 2:14 says that Hiddekel is the river that encompasses or conquers the land of Assyria. In the scripture, Assyria always represents the anti-Christ, the spirit of the anti-Christ and the agenda of the anti-Christ. This is not just talking about something to be manifest at the end of the age. Anti-Christ is all around us. You have been contending with the spirit of anti-Christ all your life whether you realize it or not. John says this in 1 John 4:3:

[1Jo 4:3 KJV] 3 And every spirit that confesseth not that Jesus Christ is come in the flesh is not of God: and this is that [spirit] of antichrist, whereof ye have heard that it should come; and even now already is it in the world.

Do you have circumstances, people or situations in your life that are resisting the Lordship of Christ? Do you have the transparency of heart to acknowledge character flaws and attitudes in your own person from time to time that manifest when you yourself are under pressure that militate against the Spirit of Christ and what obedience to God should look like at the time? That is the spirit of anti-Christ even in your own character rearing its rebellion against God. What is God's solution to this? His solution springs from the river of God that He has placed on the inside of you, in your human spirit that is designed to give you the strength to conquer everything on the inside of you and in your outward life that opposes the heart of God. You see you must conquer the inward territory of your heart before you will ever consistently see blessing and victory in your outward circumstances. Solomon made this statement:

[Pro 16:32 KJV] 32 He that ruleth his spirit than he that taketh a city.

Inward conquest brings outward victory. When the walls on the inside of you resisting the work of God in your inner man fall, then the outward opposition of the enemy in your life, your marriage, your job, your ministry will crumble. You can mount this assault and take bridgehead after bridgehead of carnality and worldliness in your character, but until you topple the anti-Christ strongholds in the depths of your being it will be an unending war. Paul put it this way:

[2Co 10:5 KJV] 5 Casting down imaginations, and every high thing that exalteth itself against the knowledge of God, and bringing into captivity every thought to the obedience of Christ;

Please realize that this verse in 2 Corinthians speaks in its totality of things that are on the inside of you in your character, your personality, and your make up. Spiritual warfare "OUT THERE" somewhere is a religious figment and fantasy until you conquer the strongholds of Satan in your own flawed character. There are imaginations in you that consistently exalt themselves against the knowledge of God. There are high things in you - like the high places and the groves of ancient Israel where the pagan idols were worshiped, inward idolatries that resist the supremacy and the lordship of Christ in your life. How do you defeat them? By opening up the floodgates of God on the inside of your human spirit until your belly (John 7:37-39) releases the rivers of God to inundate your will, your mind and your emotions bringing them into captivity to Christ.

The anti-Christ spirit is not just something that is to come, it is on the earth already. It will not only profane the temple that will be in the end time, it profanes and seeks to profane the temple that you are today. How does he do this? Paul describes the enemy's activity in the temple that you are in 2 Thessalonians:

[2Th 2:4 KJV] 4 Who opposeth and exalteth himself above all that is called God, or that is worshipped; so that he as God sitteth in the temple of

God, shewing himself that he is God.

The anti-Christ spirit is that influence that puts our thoughts before God's thoughts, our plans before God's plans and our wants before God's purposes. How do we defeat him? In Gen. 2:14 the name of the Hiddekel river means "the rushing river..." What does that speak to us as a weapon of warfare against the anti-Christ? The word "Assyria" that typifies the anti-Christ spirit means to be "level" or "right". Solomon tells us twice in the book of Proverbs:

[Pro 14:12 KJV] 12 There is a way which seemeth right unto a man, but the end thereof [are] the ways of death.

You have to make a choice between being right or being obedient to God. You cannot deliberate slowly you must RUSH (Hiddekel) to obedience our you won't make it. Example: Are you going to follow common sense, level-minded thinking (Assyria/Anti-Christ) and what you think is right or you are going to obey God? Obeying God is about making the 7-second decision. Don't think - just DO. God's thoughts are not our thoughts. He thinks faster than we do. If we are going to keep up with God we are going to have to jettison our rationale, what we think is right, what we think is a level-headed decision and simply obey God. The Hiddekel - the RUSHING RIVER defeats the spirit of Anti-Christ. The enemy cannot trip up or misdirect the believer who hears from God and obeys without hesitation.

There was nothing level headed about Noah building an ark of salvation for over 100 years against a threat that had never existed before.

There was nothing level headed about Abraham leaving his homeland and moving into enemy territory because of an ancient promise to his bloodline.

There was neither anything level headed about Abraham taking a knife and wood to sacrifice Isaac at the behest of an inward voice that spoke to him to do so.

There was nothing level headed about Jacob thinking he was going to outwrestle the angel of God but it produced a breakthrough in his life that saved him and his family from the murderous rage of Esau.

There was nothing level headed about Gideon going up against 100,000 Midianites with 300 men.

There was nothing level headed about Shadrach, Meshach and Abednego taunting the king and getting thrown into a fiery furnace but they came out without even the smell of smoke on their clothes.

I assure you that Shadrach Meshach and Abednego

did not launch a feasibility study to determine whether or not being thrown into the fiery furnace was going to work out for them. They rushed headlong into obedience to God and then they received their miracle.

Stop thinking and just let the river of God, the rushing river of the mind of God and the thoughts of God take you to the breakthrough in life you have cried out for. God is not going to bring a breakthrough in your life or ministry on your terms or on your timetable or according to your idea of how you think it is going to happen. However, if you will obey without hesitation the leading of the Spirit you will propel yourself into your NOW and see God do things in a MOMENT of TIME that you thought would take years to accomplish.

We aren't talking about being brash or foolish. We are talking about something flowing up out of your spirit and communicating itself to your waking mind of the river of God that militates against the spirit of anti-Christ trying to destroy your future. You cannot eat from the tree of the knowledge of Good and Evil. You cannot take time to weigh things out - you MUST obey promptly and then you will see the outcomes that God promised you in life, in your marriage, in your finances, your job, and your ministry. It's all about:

Do what you see the Father do (John 5:19)

Have no opinion about the consequences (Matt. 7:1)

Relinquish the outcome (John 12:24)

This is the definitive expression of denying yourself and following Jesus. This is the path to the 100 fold return in your life of the things of God. Prompt obedience without hesitation like Peter getting out of the boat against the advice of 11 of the most spiritual people in his life. There are waters of adversity that God is inviting you to walk on. Jesus is bidding you come. Don't think - just do and you as well will have your own personal water walking testimony. The rushing river, or the spiritual meaning of Hiddekel points to the fact that when you simply say "yes" to God you are moving at the pace of an uncreated being. Satan is a created being and he cannot keep up, catch up or out think you when you are saying yes to God promptly without deliberation, as Jesus "your doctrine" or "thoughts" are not your own, but His and suddenly everything you say and do becomes as effective as if the Father said it or did it!

THE FOURTH AND FINAL RIVER - THE EUPHRATES:

The final river mentioned in Genesis 2 is the

Euphrates. The other three rivers all mention what land they "encompass" or take authority over. The Euphrates doesn't make a reference to the land where it flows because it represents the whole of the definition of God's character and blessing not just in one area but in every area of your life. "Euphrates" means "fruitful". Have you ever wondered just what it means to be fruitful in God? It means to walk in INCREASE (Pison); BREAKTHROUGH (Gihon); and PROMPT OBEDIENCE (Hiddekel) in such a way that you dominate the cyclical spiral of lack and downturn (Havilah), and breakthrough the darkness that seeks to encroach your life (Ethiopia); walking in total and prompt obedience, manifesting God's glory and truth in your life through a testimony of full blessing, absolute dividend in God as His character and personality shine through the pure, clear waters of your soul in total submission to His thought and will from this day to the last day of your earthly sojourn. Even so - LORD JESUS!

ABOUT THE AUTHOR

Russ Walden is a prophet and marketplace minister with over 30 years of service in the Kingdom of God. Russ and Kitty founded Father's Heart Ministry in 2007 and since then have prophesied to tens of thousands in 78 countries and all seven continents.

Russ was born again in 1967 and called to the ministry in 1972 through an open vision of the cross and the throne of God. He served as a full time pastor to several congregations congregations in his early years before launching into a global prophetic ministry.

In the early 90's Russ participated in the oversight of a group of 400 churches before founding an IT business in the Mid-west. Russ and his wife Kitty converted the business to a marketplace ministry model and out of that Father's Heart Ministry was born.

In the prophetic ministry Russell's life has given witness to many creative miracles, healings and two resurrections from the dead. Russ has seen cancers and terminal diseases reversed through the power of prayer and the gifts of the Spirit. The ministry that Russ moves in is not just talking "about" Jesus but manifesting and activating the demonstration of Spirit and the demonstration of God's power.

Each day Prophet Russ releases a powerful prophetic word that encourages thousands. Russ brings a new dimension of personal empowerment to the prophetic through his dynamic and positive anointing. Russ flows in prophetic wisdom drawn from a lifetime of revelatory inquiry into the deep things of God.

Russ and his wife Kitty have a passion to raise up a relevant prophet generation through mentoring, prophetic schools, and personal ministry as they travel throughout the world. (For more information visit www.propheticnow.com)

Made in the USA
Columbia, SC
05 September 2020

18008200R00057